THE
LIFE OF A
MORRIS MINOR
NAMED MOGGY

THE LIFE OF A MORRIS MINOR NAMED MOGGY

HIS
RESTORATION

(RESURRECTION)

IN ENGLAND AND DOWN UNDER

ON EMIGRATION TO AUSTRALIA & BACK

Gerald Griffiths

authorHOUSE®

The photo's belong to Gerald Griffiths
and are copyright to him

The complete Graphical designs
of all the pages,and typing
by Gerald Glyn Griffiths.

AuthorHouse™
1663 Liberty Drive
Bloomington, IN 47403
www.authorhouse.com
Phone: 1-800-839-8640

Published by AuthorHouse   02/08/2013

ISBN: 978-1-4817-8126-8 (sc)
ISBN: 978-1-4817-8127-5 (e)

Foreword
By
Phil Knickenberg

I would like to thank Gerald, (Moggy) for allowing me to write a foreword for their book, Gerald has written this story for Moggy as he is writing it in the third party, as if Moggy is telling the story himself, Moggy being what his Pet car name is. It is a great tribute to Classic cars, especially to the Classic Morris Minor, I must say that this is a wonderful pictorial dictating it's restoration and the complete life story of Moggy, It is a wonderful read from a family man who shows kindness and consideration to everyone he meets.

I am in partnership with a close friend, 'Tony Conforti' and we run a Panel beating firm for crash cars. I am very pleased to have been involved with the restoration of this Lovely Morris Minor. As you will see Gerald had to work hard on the Preparation of the car, as we were not able to find time between crash repairs to do it for him.

I agreed to allow Gerald to use the workshop, for him to do this work and showed him what to do, the photos in the book will tell you how hard he worked and how Moggy was restored.

This Moggy is one of the most travelled cars that I have ever heard of, what with it immigrating to Australia and back, 'Moggy's Life is a Great read'.

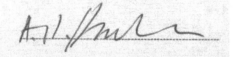

Signed by Phil Knickenberg

I have put this sign in, to thank Phil for all he has done.

ELMORE COURT   ELMORE
QUEDGELEY GLOUCESTER ENGLAND

Photo by Gareth Hughes

Gerald Glyn Griffiths, the Writer

(Author)

'Moggy' The Morris Minor the Author

(The story Teller)

The Book is Dedicated To

Ernest Griffiths, the Authors Uncle, and to Ernie's son, John Griffiths, to John Griffiths's Wife Teresa Griffiths and to their two Daughters, Ellen and Leanne, hopefully it will be a fantastic keepsake for their children, also to all the Griffiths's and their families of generations to come.

This photo is when the Author's Mum and Dad visited the Griffiths family
On their wedding day, 5th June 1934. At Blackwood South Wales.
Granddad Thomas Bryant Griffiths front left,
At the Back left to right: My uncle Alf, Sister Ruth, Aunty May, Cousin Jean.
My Dad, and behind him is Miss Lewis, who at that time was their Servant. My Mum,

Uncle Ernest, on her right,
Then my Grandmother Elizabeth Emanuel Griffiths.

CONTENTS

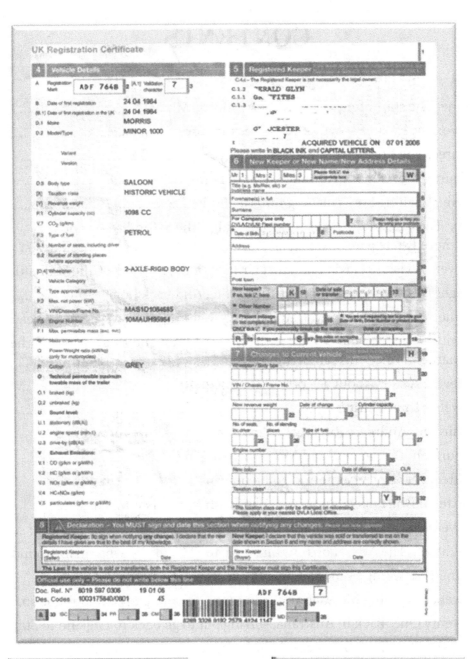

Vehicle Inspectorate

Crystal Mark

Clarity
approved by
Plain English Campaign

MOT test certificate

Motor vehicle registration mark   ADF 764B

This certificate has been issued according to the conditions and notes on the back of this certificate.

Note: If you have doubts as to whether this certificate is valid, call our MOT enquiry line on: **0845 600 5977**.

Vehicle identification
or chassis number: 1064683

Test station number: 81908

Colour of vehicle: GREY

Issue date: APRIL 01ST 2003
ZERO - THREE

Make of vehicle: MORRIS

Approximate year the
vehicle was first used: 1964

Expiry date: MARCH 31ST 2004
ZERO - FOUR

Recorded mileage: 34033

If it is a goods vehicle,
state the maximum
design gross weight: N/a

Serial number of the
last test certificate: N/a

Type of fuel: PETROL

For all vehicles
with more than
8 passenger seats

Seat belt installation
checked this test?
(tick if appropriate)   Yes ✓

Previous installation check date: N/a

Number of seat belts fitted at
time of installation check

Tester's signature:

Tester's name in CAPITALS: A. TANDY

Warning
A test certificate is not evidence that the
vehicle is in a satisfactory mechanical condition.

Check
Check carefully that the above details are correct.
Do not accept a certificate which has been altered.

Serial number:

GPO557653

Authentication stamp

ROBERT TIMMS
CAINCROSS ROAD GARAGE
STROUD 763229/763150
V.T.S. NO. 81908

Produced by SPSL 4153   VT20 (06/02)

ELMORE COURT, GLOUCESTER, ENGLAND

This is the Story of a Morris Minor 1000 Saloon, the date of its first registration was 24th April 1964, and its Engine Cylinder capacity is 1098. It is now classed as a Historical Vehicle

Moggy's first Registration

NUMBER PLATE ADF 764

The first owner was a Mr Ernest Griffiths or Ernie as he was called, who was my Dad's brother. Sadly Ernie died on the 28th March 1982, and Moggy was left in his will to his son, 'John Griffiths'. Sadly John Griffiths died on 19th October 2005, and his Wife Teresa Griffiths left it in my care, giving it to me after John's funeral, this was on a promise that I would look after it and keep it in the Family.

This is a Photo of my Uncle Ernest, when he was young around they age of twenty. He always had a love of the Morris Minor as he was growing up, and in those days it was classed as a working-class man's car. I do believe he purchase about three of these car's, the Morris named Moggy was the last one he bought and he had it up until the day he died. I do know that he was very musical and was a member of the Salvation Army, and played an instrument.

John Griffiths his son in this photo taken 1962—64 was also very musical, and played a wind instrument, the Cornet, he was a very accomplished player. John's wife had told me that John had played at Royal Albert Hall in London and had a standing ovation. John's Mum was called Alice, but she Died when John was very young, and in later years around 1964 John's Dad remarried again to a very nice Lady called Dorothy which you can see on page 72.

John and his family nick-named it 'MOGGY', and from 1982 till 2005 John and John's wife used this car constantly. John's two Girls, Ellen and Leanne cherished this car, knowing it was their Father's and Grandfather's Car. Because of this I really felt that I had a strong responsibility to look after it.

I will say no more as MOGGY wishes' to tell the story of his life himself.

CHAPTER ONE

WELL HERE WE GO

I WILL HAND YOU OVER TO,

THE MORRIS MINOR CALLED

MOGGY

The Start of my life as Moggy (Morris)

ADF 764 B—Morris 1000, Saloon

Well, 'hey everyone', I am going to start my story right from the very beginning when I was born, (Manufactured) on the 24th April 1964, My full model type name is Morris 1000, and I am a saloon, and of course I would be classed as a historic vehicle of today, 2010. My actual Cylinder capacity is 1098 CC, I use petrol but because of petrol being unleaded now, I now have to have a special fluid mixed in the petrol which helps keep my heart (engine) ticking over more cleanly.

I was then adopted, (bought) in that same year and the first registration in the UK was 24th April 1964. The man that adopted (bought), me was named Mr Ernie Griffiths he lived in Stroud not far away from where I was born (Manufactured). I would like to say since I was born, I have been a well travelled Car of the world. And have been down under in Oz 'Australia' for two years, but now I am back in good old Blighty, where I have so many friends and relatives that love me so much, and to be able to see Teresa and the girls Leanne and Ellen, I will tell you all about my life starting with my home in Stroud in 1964.

Mr Ernie Griffiths, Moggy's first owner

This was to become my home here in Stroud for the next forty-four years, and Ernie was a very kind man and he took me to the Doctors, (*Morris Minor Centre*) on a regular basis for Checkups, (service) I would have a blood transfusion, (*oil Change*) and all my veins and arteries (*Clutch & brake pipes*) toped up with fluid. My heart (*Engine*) was also checked very regularly and tuned to perfection; I found I could run forever, 'very smoothly'.

I have all the Certificates, and papers, and records, to prove it to this very day. When I came of the showroom, I was very proud of myself, 'I gleamed', and I was immaculate. I was a grey dull, but bright colour, which was quite fashionable of the day.

On the down side, Ernie was a terrible driver, he has given me quite a few scare's over the years. I remember once he was going to drive down to Bristol from Gloucester taking his Nephew and Niece Gerald and Angela Griffiths; Gerald being the author of this Book, 'who is writing this for me'. He was picking them up at Slimbridge, and on coming out of Slimbridge to the crossroad, which was a Carriageway, he turned right strait away without crossing over to the left hand side of the carriageway, I was so frightened and I could do nothing about it, as Ernie had control of me, and was holding the stirring wheel so tight. His passengers were scared stiff, and shouted at him to stop, 'you are going down the wrong side of the carriageway Ernie', they said.

He went to the correct left hand side of the road, and we thought we were sooo Sooo lucky nothing was coming the other way, and we got away with it, Because of this his son, 'John Griffiths', Gerald Griffiths's cousin, learnt to drive at a very young age, he use to drive me for him, so over the years I was always thankful, when John did the driving.

The photo on the right is Ernie with his son John and Mary, 'Gerald's sister' and as you can see John looks quite young in this picture and at this age he was all ready driving me, his Dads car even at this early age, probably around fourteen.

Incidentally Mary died at an early age at 44 years old on 11th April 1991. Gerald was devastated, Gerald would say she was such fun loving girl to be with, and she left two lovely daughters Sarah and Vicky, Vicky had a daughter only a few months after Mary past away, and she did not get to see her. 'That was so sad'.

Sadly the 28th March in the year 1982 Ernie past away and John Griffiths inherited me as part of his Dads estate, I was very fortunate as John love's me as much as his Dad did, and tried to keep me together as much as he could. The years started to take its toll though and John found it hard to get some of the jobs done correctly. In England you have to have what they call an MOT which is where every year I had to go over a pit, everything had to be checked, and be made road worthy, what with winter's in the UK the road would get salted and gritted to stop you sliding and skidding on the ice and snow. With the bad winters we had been having there was a lot of salt getting into my metalwork, so I started to deteriorate.

But John managed to keep me on the road. He had to give me four new wheel arches, because my old ones had rusted right through, 'what with the salt and everything'. He never got around to getting the wheel arches sprayed. I really did need a heavy makeover, but it was not happening.

I do know John kept me clean and tidy and I was garaged all the time, and I felt quite secure in the knowledge that John loved me, mostly because I belonged to his Dad.

His wife Teresa loved me to, and she knew that John cherished me and would love to have been able to get me completely restored.

Sadly that was not to be as John had a long illness and passed away on the 19th October of the year 2005.

There were so many people at his funeral as he was so well liked, 'at work and home'. Gerald, a cousin loved John and I do know that even though they did not see enough of each other. Gerald and John had a very good relationship and a special bond between them. Gerald was there at the funeral and got talking to Teresa, John's wife and his two young girls Ellen and Leanne about the happy time's and was reminiscing about me and John and his Dad Ernie.

It got around to what would be happening to me, and if I was going to be put back on the road, she said she has someone who was willing to have me and she was going to let me go, Gerald said he would be willing to buy me off her, so as to keep me in the family. She agreed to this, but said if you look after him you can have him and she did not want anything for me. And now I was being adopted, by John's cousin, 'Gerald'.

He promise to look after me, and see if he could do me up a bit, and a couple of months later, on the 19th December 2005 he came to take me home to his place, this all happened very quickly as Teresa was sad at having to let and see me go.

This is me when I first got there at Gerald's, all covered over with a blue tarpaulin

Gerald lived on a large property on a canal, and I was put up the side of a garage with a cover over me to keep me dust free and dry. At first I felt warm and safe but as the months went by, and Gerald had not given me any attention. I started to feel unwanted and unloved; I started to feel quite depressed. Months went into years; I started to feel as if I was dying myself. I could feel the cold and the rust eating away at my metal. I wish old Ernie was here to help me, if John could see me now he would be so unhappy.

As you can see it is nice here, and look at the Beautiful Ship going by his house,
but I was not getting to see any of it because of being shut away.

This is me where the cover has blown off and I am left to the elements. You can see my poor rust sore's up the side of my doors panels' and along the bottom of my sills but what you can't see is my floor, which is very bad, and my lovely grill is no longer that. 'As that has got rusty to'. I am really down in the dumps.

I was getting tired of this as I was not getting used and my joint's were beginning to get stiff from lack of use, if only Gerald would take me out for a drive that would be good, but it was not happening. I did get moved a couple of time's but only from one end of the garden to the other,

This is me just being moved around the garden again. And under the blue tarpaulin.

This is Gerald's place from the air, and you can see the blue tarpaulin covering me, up along the house.

During this time, Gerald had been working on his garden, and in it he had about seven or eight, forty foot conifers growing in there, and I felt very vulnerable in the position I was, as I felt a bit too close to them when he was felling them. Thank god he moved me when he got to the last few. You can see how big they are, and how close I was in these pictures

Well it is the year 2008, Gerald has had me now for over three years, and he has done nothing for me, so much for his promises to Teresa, after when she was so kind enough to give me to him. Anyway it is a nice morning today I think it is around about June or July, with warmer weather. Gerald is coming down the garden towards me looks as though he has a battery charger in his handw. I thought wow he's going to get me going, perhaps take me out for a spin. Well I am fully charged now and Gerald, still had a lot of trouble starting me after such a long time of standing, but he got me going and is now driving me out of the gate, and down the road he did not go far, maybe a few yards turned around and took me back, I was gutted, but I did learn that I was not Taxed so that was why he did not go right out of his road.

On the day of the 8th June 2008, He did start to wash me and I felt cleaner than I have ever had for some time, and I began to feel that something was in the air, he had turned me around and I was facing the gate, he left me alone for a while and then this big van and a trailer, came in the drive, It had big writing on the side of the van, it said Morris Minor centre, I thought Fxxc I know that company, it was The Charles Wares, Morris Minor Centre from Bristol, in Brislington.

Incidentally, 'I did here that that was where Gerald Griffiths was born and brought up in Brislington Bristol'. This was the same company that Ernie used to take me to, but in those days they were stationed in Bath. Well because Gerald had not paid me much attention over the last few years I thought the worse, 'he was getting rid of me'. But then I heard them talking to Andy Hemming's which was the man's name and Gerald said to him, 'if you can give me a fair price on a restoration', and what has to be done, he would go ahead with it, they shook hands and then I was put on to the trailer.

I thought whoopee; I am going to be resurrected (restored).
On arriving at The Charles Wares Centre in Bristol I could see their big sign and lots of Morris Minors out the front, of all the different colours and models, I was so excited, Gerald was going ahead with it, he was going to get me a makeover.

The Charles Wares Centre of no 20 Clothier Road Brislington Bristol BS4 5PS.
This is the first thing you see when you drive down Clothier road on the right.

Well I was then off loaded into their back yard, where lots of other cars and van were. There were Morris Minor traveller's which has the wooden frame, and some very old mates that had a split windscreens and as I was able to look around, I managed to recognise some of my old friends that I have met over the years, even a mate that I knew who was used in the TV series Heart Beat, he became a police car in Heart beat I hope I will be able to chat over good times with him as well.

This is Gerald's Wife, 'June', and a Morris Traveller with the wood trims then a Morris 1000 which looks just the same as me.

CHAPTER TWO

The Charles Ware's Morris Minor Centre was founded in Bath, UK in 1976. They moved to Bristol in 2006 in order to consolidate all their workshops and stores under one roof. For 35 years they have provided a specialised service in the restoration, care and repair of the Morris Minor. They stock a complete range of new and used Morris Minor parts and spares and have unrivalled experience in the mail order supply to Minor owners worldwide.

Moggy introducing you To the Morris Minor centre.

These are more of the cars outside waiting for repair; The Mini must be a Morris Mini.

More car's out the back see the white Morris Van, then a Morris 1000 like me then an open top.

This is my Mate I wanted you to see, he is the one that was in Heart Beat on TV in Britain. And now televised all over the world

The Start of Moggy's Makeover.

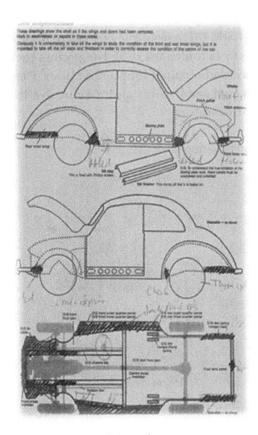

On the day of the 11ᵗʰ June 2009 my diagnoses was confirmed and Gerald was notified.

The diagnoses of my body parts were quite sever there is a lot to be done, see the diagnoses paper on the left.

I have just found out that Gerald is concerned of how much it is going to cost, as they have told him there is so much to be done, so all my excitment at the begining when I left home, after hearing Gerald say he would have me restored, it looked as though I had jumped the gun.

Things are looking bad, all the things and final estimate has come in, and I have to have welding to the Chassia and replace front and rear floor pans and the centre of my offside and my front floor pan on my near side, they all have to be replaced. The cross member ends have to be replaced. Even my doors have to be repaired with new panels, a lot of mechanical work, and my engine serviced, all my brakes has got to be renewed including four front wheel cylinders, two rear wheel cylinders, all of my brake shoes, the list is endless.

I am becoming quite scared, as I dont think Gerald may not want to go ahead with it, as it is so expensive, even though Mr Andy Hemings would be giving a good bit of discount I am still afraid, Gerald may have me scrapped, and sent to the scrap-yard in the sky.

The centre are waiting for Gerald to get back to them for the go ahead. It's now a Friday and I just dont want to be waiting all the weekend for Gerald to make up his mind, anyway as I was just thinking this, Mr Andy Hemings, came into the work shop and told his machanics to start work on me, Yahoooooo, we are away, lets go.

Well this is it I have had my wheel arches ampitated (removed) and they have been preparing me for surgery, by removing windscreen and bumper and they have put me back outside for a while

This is me out there with my Mates.

I think I am going in tomrrow for Major surgery. There will be a lot of floor cut out then replaced, this is there surgery where it all happens. First picture, a Traveller having worked done, second picture another Traveller having work done on the engine, third & forth picture just being put back together. The rest of the pictures are from the room where they are finished and ready for collection of their owners, or some that are sold.

This is me, 'Moggy', you cant see me properly, as they have me on my side ready for the work.

As you can see it looks bad, and they have already cut out some of the chassis in the front

You can now see it's me, and they are now working on me.

You can see the welder working on me, it doe's not hurt, and I did not need to be anaseticnised.

As you can see I have had different experts working on me, and they are all doing a good job.

You can see the new Left and right pans.

These pictures are where the springs join the body, chassis back and front, the new chassis panels

Here you can see my new floor and the new panes.

Well here I am back outside again, I do feel better and stronger but I don't feel any more beautiful, I still look the same as when I came here. God, will I ever look like my showroom self again.

I am so disappointed. I have heard I am off back to Gloucester; I thought they were going to make me Beautiful. I can't believe I still look the same. Mr Andy Heming's is taking me back at this very moment but we have past Gerald's house and district, and going right into Gloucester.

We have arrived at a Panel beating firm, and I can see their name over the door. The Gloster Motor Repairs, Fxxk, if this is where I will be having more work done, I hope they know what they are doing they can't even spell Gloucester right.

Back outside again awaiting what happens next

Well I am here, and they have started on me

CHAPTER THREE

The Cosmetic Surgery of Moggy

So here I am at The Gloucester Motor Repairs, 'see we can spell it right': Well I do realise now I am nowhere near finished, and that the repairs I have already, have had, was internal surgery (Mechanical repairs) I am so glad about that as I thought, that was that and I would never look like I did as when I was new and in the show room.

I have heard the owners of the panel beating company talking to Gerald, and I realise that they are close friends. Gerald is a Martial arts Instructor of Mr Philip Knickenberg one of the partners 'Oh yes', I forgot to tell you that Gerald has practiced and taught Karate and Martial Arts for over forty years, 'nearly fifty'. Mr Philip Knickenberg partner's name is, Mr Tony Conforti. Apparently they have a very good reputation, so there work load is quite heavy, and I could hear when they were talking, due to the work load Philip would only take me on, if Gerald did all the preparation of rubbing down ECT, for the paint job.

Gerald said he would be happy to do so, he said it would bring him closer to me, and knowing that I did belong to John his Cousin and his uncle Ernie, he would be able to take pride in doing it for them both. I thought back to how I felt when Gerald was ignoring me and leaving me out in his garden all that time, when I thought that he did not care, I realised he did care, and that he was doing his best.

He was pulling out all the stops, and I know the amount he has already spent on me so far, so I do appreciate what he is doing, and now know he loves me just as much as his Uncle Ernie and John did, 'his Cousin'. Gerald has started the work the following day after I got there, as they were expecting me and everything was arranged.

Next day, Gerald did not turn up until about ten o'clock, he started his tea-brake strait away, 'I thought yes typical', and he can't even get out of bed, and was not an early riser. To have a tea brake strait away, was not on, as I was waiting to get started. After his tea brake he got stuck in to me. He did need supervisory supervision, as he was not talented on this sort of work, but he was a fast learner and soon got going. Here are some picture of him working on me, and Mr Knickenberg and Mr Conforti showing him how.

He has just finished covering my window openings and the glass on my doors.

As you see in the last two pictures.

As you can see Tony and Phil is showing Gerald what to do and how to use the machnery

As you can see, I have had a bit of work done, and Gerald now knows what to do, so they are going to leave him to it.

Gerald is realy getting into it now and on day three he has taken my grill, and my bumpers back and front bonnet and boot door and removed them all, and covered my engine with paper so paint wont got on my engine. So as to get right underneath he is now rubbing all my parts down on a bench, Then over the next week he has to work on my wings, rubbing and sanding them down. Everything seems to be going well, and I am please with what he is doing.

Phil filling in the doors after they were all sanded and rubbed down, and showing gerald what to do. Everything is looking good so far, Gerald seems to be helping me look good with much more love and affection, and I am beginning to fill much more wanted. I can see Gerald and Mr Phillip knickenberg are great friends and I certainly know Gerald really appreciats phil, for allowing him to do all this at his work shop.

Phil and his partner said, to have a car in the premises on this scale with this amount of preperation. is not profitable for there business, You can see the amount of work that is being done, and a vehicle that would be taking up room for this long, would be hindering there fast turnover on crashed cars. But Phil kindly agreed to do this because they are best friends and Gerald was willing to do most of this preperation.

As you can see my wing's have been brought right back to the bare metal, Gerald is doing a proper job, he is a bit of a perfectionis, when it comes to things like this, I will take back all I said about him, 'he's Great'.

 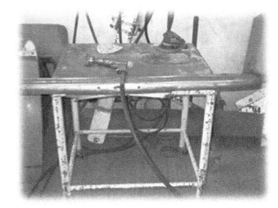

Bottom of doors being rubbed down by Gerald and working from a bench on the two Vallances back and front and the both Bar Mountings.

You can see how well my two Vallences are looking and Gerald painted the backs of them with a very expencive metal paint which kills all rust, called Hamerite. Even behind the Chrome Bumper Blades. Also all the inside of my Boot has been painted with this same special paint. ----

I have been here a couple of weeks now and Gerald has rubbed down all those parts of me and now, is waiting for all my body to be primed, as we agreed with Phil and Tony they could only do it when they have time between doing their normal Jobs. What Gerald has been doing while waiting, is all the little bits and pieces that would not have been done if a garage had agreed to do the whole job?.

What he has been doing at the moment is my boot and giving it a good going over, with that special paint he has, he also made a new wooden panel for the shelf in my boot, which was beautifully made and varnished. My boot looked amazing what with a nice new mat and everything he had done.

While Gerald is working on me, Phil and Tony has to carry on working on there crash cars, that are coming in all the time, you see Phil here in these pictures working on the door of a crashed car.

Phil fixing on some lights.

Tony working on a bumper.

All sanded down and ready for first primer. Bottom picture left, Tony is covering the wheels with paper, so they don't get paint on them. Phil is just doing a bit more rubbing down on a missed bit. Well here we go, next few pictures I am having my Car Body primed, more work for Gerald.

Tony now spraying the Primer for my first rub down, then sprayed with green fleck.

In this next picture, my parts, you see are my Bonnet and Boot cover and on the top of the car are all my Bumper Valences and Chrome Bumper Blades and Grill Panel that has had its first primer. Gerald has to rub it all down again ready for the first undercoat. As he rubs me down none of the green flecks must show.

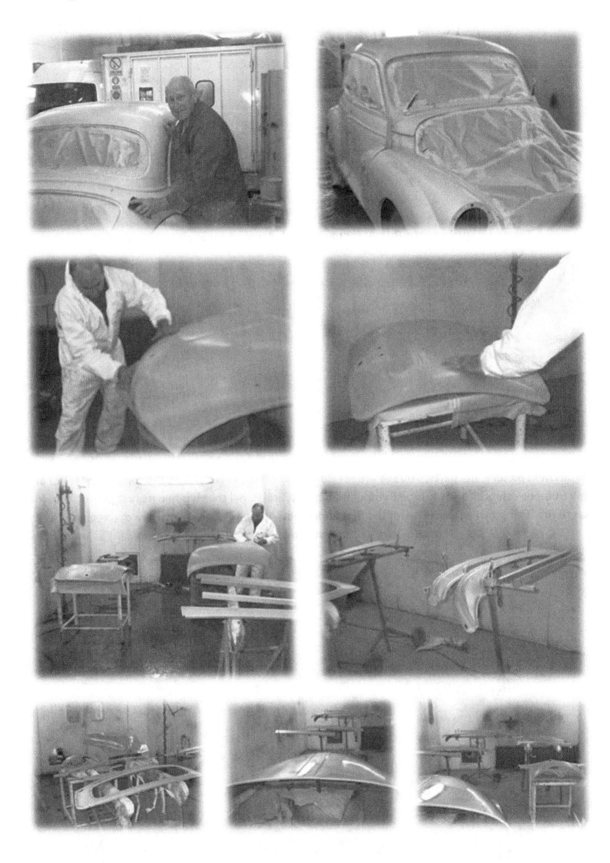

In the back ground you can see my bonnet with its first coat of paint and my Bumper Valances in the foreground, ready for painting, and all these parts of me will have to be rubbed down again. But I am sure Gerald is up to it, I heard Phil telling Tony that he is doing a good job.

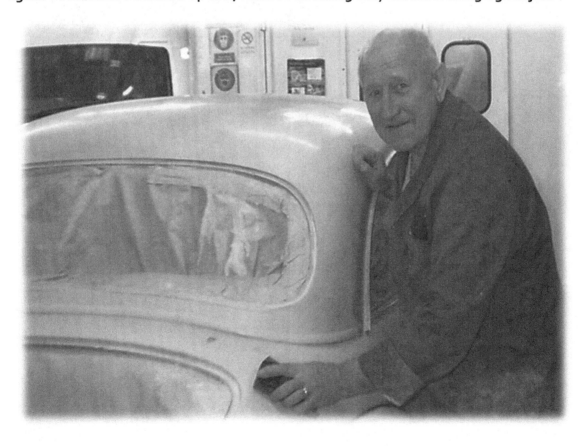

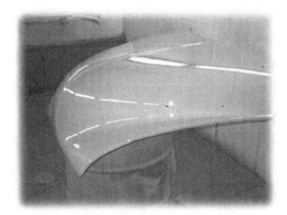

'The last coat has been done'. Everything is ready now for my bodyparts to be put back together, as all my painting on my body has been done, and Phil and Tony are about to get on with it. The first two pictures is my bonnet boot cover, On the next couple of pages is the Last touches of being back together, and more polishing ECT;

All is looking good, and I am feeling so fresh and clean I am gettinwg beautiful.

The Grill about to go on.

My grill is done, going to get my eyes (*headLight's*) put back in.

This picture is Phil putting my eyes (*headlights*) back in.

Photo of Tony seeing to my bonnet, Then more polishing ECT;

I really fill that I am now back to my Showroom best, except for my wheels, to which Gerald has gone to Bristol to get me new one's from the Charles Ware's Morris Minor Centre, then I am complete. But the polishing goes on; Tony is meticulously doing such a grand job.

v

Phil messing around, he will not really hit me with that sledge hammer.
And Phil and Tony posing for the camera

Well Gerald has even painted all around my heart (*engine*) mountings and has cleaned my heart and renewed my artery to my fuel pipes and painted my radiator.

Phil and Tony posing with me outside their factory, it was such a privilege meeting them, and I would like to thank them from the bottom of my heart (*Engine*) for helping Gerald in Resurrecting (*Restoration'ing*) me.

Here is Phil standing by me just before Gerald is going to drive me home. 'June', Gerald's wife is sitting in my passenger seat waiting to go home,

Just setting off to Gerald's home, at the Rea Bridge House.

CHAPTER FOUR

A few photos of me
posing in and around
Gerald's Garden at the Rea Bridge House

This is me posing with Gerald and June's new Mercedes. 2009.

Now that Gerald has spent so much on me looking good, I am now garaged.

I am posing with my doors open showing how good I am looking.

As you can see, my entire interior has been cleaned and the seats have had all the vinyl restored.

Gerald and June are going to go out for a drive, because now that I am all looking like a new Car, he is so proud of me, and wants to show me off.
Bottom photo, waiting to cross the Canal at the Rea Bridge.

CHAPTER FIVE

A Sailing Ship crashing into the Bridge

This is the Ship we were waiting for, and it actually crash's into the bridge, and as an ex-Bridgeman Gerald was allowed on the bridge and the picture's he took on the bridge shows the impact, we had to wait awhile for the bridge to close.

The Ship Earl of Pembroke was returning from Weymouth for the Gloucester tall Ships festival. The Ship had caught a gust of wind as it approached the Rea Bridge. This picture show's after impact and you can see the snapped off bowsprit hanging into the water The next pictuer is when it arrived in the Docks in Gloucester, which shows the snapped off bowsprit. David Redhead, the gereral manager of Sqauae Sail, which is a company based in Cornwall, had said that the incident would not put them back to much, accidents can happen and you just have to get on with things, and it should only take a few days to fully repair it.

These pictures' show the Earl of Pembroke in the dry dock being repaired

Two nice pictures of me at the Gloucester docks.

June Gerald's wife sitting in my Passenger seat.

CHAPTER SIX

This picture is a sailing ship the Saren Larsen from the series of the Onedin-Line, going through the bridge; The Gloucester Town Crier in top of the Mast Head in Red Jacket, Gerald is on the bridge with yellow jacket and his house is in the background; a friend of his was kind enough to take the picture for him from a street light crane, the other pictures are panoramic views of the bridge and Gerald's house and his neighbours.

This first one was around 1980; the second one was around 2007 when I arrived at Gerald's house.

Spring and winter at Rea Bridge

Gerald's took these picture's right outside his home on Canal.

Different angles on Gerald's lawn. Calling at Elmore court for a photo, then off down to see David and Janet.

This is outside the Elmore Court Manor Estate in Elmore.

CHAPTER SEVEN

David and Janet at their home in Stoke Gifford in Bristol. In the Picture with me are Gerald's Brother David and his wife Janet with June. 2009'.

I do know that as Gerald is typing this part of my story he is very sadden, as all though this is a part of my life in 2009. At this very moment of typing it is the year 2011 and he is mourning the loss of his Brother David who died on the 2nd of November 2011 and his funeral is on this coming Monday 14th of November.

So these pictures are so Poignant for Gerald to see and is finding it hard to tell this part of the story.

These pictures were included in the book for over a year and Gerald is now filling in the gaps with his typing.

Me 'Moggy', posing with David and Janet Griffiths.

Gerald has left these photo's in this part of the book, as Gerald feels that this is a part of contributing to the memory of David and being able to look at these pictures with pride of a wonderful Brother as everyone who knew him will remember him.

Gerald wanted so much to have been at his funeral, but personal things were happening in his life in Australia that he had no control over and could not be there. Tracy his Daughter said there was over three hundred people with standing room only, and the amount of personal tributes that was read out for David was overwhelming, this is a man that stands out among men and that Gerald is so proud to call him Brother.

God Bless, R.I.P. Love you Brother David.

This is me having my picture taken with David's Daughter, Julie,
outside her home in Stoke Gifford.

David and Janet had three wonderful Daughters, Annette, Julie, and Tracy, and six wonderful Grandchildren, which are 'Harvey', 'Frazer', 'Harriet, 'Tom and Joe', and they are all living within easy reach of each other.

This picture I think was taken at the Stroud registry office when Uncle Ernie
and Dorothy wed in 1964.

In this picture from left to right. Back row Janet and David my brother, then middle row is my
brother Peter, Mum and Dad then Uncle Ernie and his wife Dorothy, in the front row is Annette
and Julie, Janet and David's two girls they have another daughter called Tracy, but she is not in
this picture, as Janet was Pregnant with her at that time, as this picture was taken around 1964,
which was the same year I was Born (*Manufactured*), and owned by Gerald's Uncle Ernie.

Now just behind the group you can just see the top of me and my front bumper, where Uncle
Ernie had parked me, shame that we could not see more of me as I was only just born and only
nearly a year old.

CHAPTER EIGHT

This is me and June, Gerald's Wife sitting in my passenger seat waiting outside Tesco's car park for him to come from the store after getting some flowers for Teresa, 'John Griffiths's wife', we are going to surprise her by taking me up to her home in Stonehouse. This will be a big surprise for her as she does not known how much work Gerald has had done on me, he only told her that he had tided me up a bit to be road worthy for the MOT ECT;.

It is going to be an extra surprise, as Gerald has just found out, it is her birthday and Teresa's Daughters, Ellen, and Leanne, will be there, so they will get to see me as well, what a surprise it will be.

This is Teresa when she first got to sit in my driving seat; when I first got there, she did shed a tear as she said of all her memories of her courting days when John use to pick her up in me, his Moggy, 'as they', John, Teresa, Ellen and Leanne, use to called me.

'Moggy the Morris Minor'.

Teresa on Memory lane, and I did see a slight tear as she reminisced on all her courting days with John, of course I use to go everywhewre with them as there transport, and I am sworn to secrecy and promised not to kiss and tale. It was so lovely seeing Teresa and the girls again and I promised to come and see them again as soon as Gerald will drive me to Stone house, he is quite a loving person and I do know Gerald likes to keep in touch wwith all his family and friends.

I then took her for a drive to the Shops.

This is me on another excursion to The Lady Smith's estate at Long-Ash don in Bristol. Gerald was reminiscing about when he use to work there as a Boy of sixteen on some windows on the right of the picture, and that's another story that Gerald has told in his Auto-Biography, which is soon to be published.

These pictures, Me, Gerald & June. Gerald & Sharon, a friend of our Son Graham.

Me, in Gerald's and June's garden, at 'The Rea Bridge House'.

This is 13th September two thousand and nine, and it is the big day of John's daughter Ellen's Wedding, she is getting married, to Dan Millard, Ellen was very thrilled to know she could have her Dads car, 'Me Moggy' at her wedding, I was so proud to be able to go. Ellen said it was like having her Dad there I am here in Gerald's Garden all dressed up with wedding ribbons, ready to go, I will be the Bride's-maids Car, and I am going to go to Teresa's home in Stonehouse to get the Bride's-maids, to take them to the church.

CHAPTER NINE

Now some wonderful photo's

Of

The wedding

Of

Ellen Marion Griffith's

To Dan Millard

In

Stonehouse Gloucestershire

The daughter

of John & Teresa Griffiths

And Granddaughter

Of Ernie Griffiths,

who I have been talking about in the Book,

My first owner.

Well here we go off to the Wedding.

A very beautiful photo of Teresa, looking as radiant, as the beautiful blushing Bride, 'Ellen'.

Ellen I think is the most Beautiful Bride, her smile lights up the world, and John would be so her proud of her, and I am so pleased to be there for her, knowing that I was John's, 'her Dads car'.

These photo's taken at her Mum's home in Stonehouse, just after getting ready for the Wedding, and I am waiting outside to take the Bride's maids to the Church

The Bride's Maid's getting ready. Ellen's Sister Leanne on the left and Jemma Greatly, Ellen's best friend.

That's what is taking them so long; this is Ellen's sister, 'Leanne', who is one of the Bride's Maid's. Better hurry up take her to the church before she gets pixxxd. Only joking she is as beautiful and as lovely as her sister and Mum. About time they are coming out

This photo we are now outside and both Brides' maids are with Ellen and me.

This is Leanne having a photo taken with me.

Just arrived at the Church, and everyone is waiting, it is well known the Bride can be late.

The Brides Mum Teresa, Bride Ellen and Groom Dan and the Best Man.

These pictures say it all, as you can see; they are so happy and make a wonderful couple.

The new Mr and Mrs Dan and Ellen Millard.

Such a loving photo of the Bride looking adoringly into the eyes of Dan, her new husband.

Ellen the Blushing Beautiful Bride, out-side the Church in the sunshine of a wonderful day.

Teresa Brides Mum and the Blushing Bride

Gerald was very proud to be able to have a photo taken with the Bride.

The Radiant Blushing Bride, so beautiful and relaxed now the ceremony is over, and now time for all the Wedding photographs.

All the wonderful Photos now taken and just going through the Church gates with the lovely guest throwing their confetti, then off to the Wedding reception.

Hey here I am, 'Moggy' with Gerald at my steering wheel and ready for the Brides Maids to take them to the Wedding reception, and June, Gerald Wife helping a Brides Maid

Arrived at the Wedding reception, the Wedding car and me Moggy.

I was so proud to have my Picture taken with Ellen,

As she lovingly stood next to me, and lent on my front headlights of my body

Here is Dan and Ellen looking into each other's eyes standing next to me, I am so pleased for them.

Ellen, Teresa and Leanne and me Moggy.
Don't know who the posh car is, he's to stuck up to talk to me.

Gerald, Ellen, and June, Gerald's wife, and of course me.

Here is Ellen and some of her friends, and I still managed to get in the back ground, heheh.

June, Gerald's wife, talking to Teresa's Mum, the Brides Grandmother . . .

Wedding reception, before all the guests arrived

I give you Mr. & Mrs. Ellen and Dan Millard
Moggy Love's & miss's you very much. xxx

I am in Tesco's car park, back at home in Quedgeley.

And I have now arrived at the Rea Bridge and waiting to cross over the bridge to our house,
On the other side of the canal.

The Rea Bridge, then a picture of our house

Family Car (Moggy)

We have a Morris Minor car, it is called the Moggy,
yet nothing about it is ever doggy'.
As it has all been seen to, where everthing about it is all become brand new.

As our bones are weary and sore and our pains are oh so many,
it would be good to say, we could be just like that car,
like a brand new penny

It is cleaned with love and taken very much cared of,
it also is a family car that has a story to tell all of it's own.
as days gone by and folks all admired the car's tone.

We know it was worth it having a car,
that had so many memories in our family alone,
keeping it going and keeping it strong.

As if nothing had ever been wrong.

It is cared for with love
and
polished with so much pride.
And nothing about it we would never want to hide

The Author, June M Griffiths

CHAPTER TEN

'The history and tribute to the Morris Minor'.

The Morris Minor is one of the most recognised icons of the past! I, 'Moggy', am very proud to have been part of that heritage. It is such a privilege to be still around after all these years and thanks' to Gerald's, 'Uncle Ernie' and 'John Griffiths his cousin', for looking after me so well, and of course Gerald himself for restored 'ting (Resurrecting) me I am still here and looking as good as new, as specially as we are not manufactured anymore, we were stopped being made at around 1971, which was seven years after I was born *(manufactured)*

Our history go's back as far as 1910 this is when the Morris Motor company was first started, when Mr William Morris turned his attention from bicycle manufacturing to Car production and began planning a new light car and opened in 1913 at the former Military College at Cowley in Oxfordshire, which then became one of Britain's first Million sell's and exports around the World.

The biggest launch being in London at the Earls Court Debuted Motor Show on the 20th September 1948, and over one point three million of us were manufactured between 1948 and 1971, we were designed as a two saloon also as a tour'er (*Convertible*) then a four door saloon in 1950 and in 1952 a wooden framed version estate (The *traveller*). There was three series, the MM (1948) the series 11 (1952) and finally the 1100 series 1956.

Mr Sir Alec Issigonis thought's was to combined luxury, with the vieww of having a car that was affordable for the working class people. Production continued being produced at Birmingham, and became to be known and described as the British Icon of a classical Englishness design.

Dedicated to The Charlie Ware's Centre, in Bristol, England

I do know that I do go on about the Charlie Ware's Centre a bit, but I do have a lot to thank them for, as I said earlier, the first time I went to the Centre was when Ernie Griffiths owned me and at that time they were stationed in bath, owner's came from all over the World to get there much needed part's for their car's, from the centre, and Charlie was so pleased as his company began to take off.

The actual first Morris Minor (TPE MM) with a 918 cc side valve engine which left the production line on the 8th October 1948, may have actually may gone through the Charlie Ware Centre and could still alive today, 'thanks to the centre'.

On arriving at the frontage of the Centre you are met with us, a row of Morris Minors, of different model's, all gleaming as new from the cosmetic surgery that the centre had provided.

With their lovely grills all looking as though they are smiling at you, and to quote; Mr Charlie Ware he said when he is talking to the customer's it is like a Surgeon talking to their Patience's Parents of the Morris as most customers actually give their cars a names just like me MOGGY,

I would like to say and give credit to the very skilled workers in SRI LANKA as to this day most of our parts do come from where and exported all over the World.

Designer Sir Alec Issigonis designed an-other first major creation which was the 'Morris Mini'. One other most recognised car, and Gerald had bought a brand-new one in 1965, whilst stationed in Germany whilst in the Armed forces, 'The Grenadier Guards'.

This is the Morris Mini that Gerald and his Mum are posing with twenty five years later.

CHAPTER ELEVEN

There is a story about Gerald and June and Graham that go's, I quote!

When Gerald and June came home to England with Graham there son from Germany, in 1967 Gerald was driving the Morris Mini you have just seen, and drove it all the way home. He also brought a German friend with them, and dropped her off at a Army Camp on Saulsbury-Plain, at two oclock in the morning, then went on to Gloucester.

After they had dropped her off, they called at a garage for petrol, and then drove along a road with rather sharp bends for around two or three miles. After coming out of these bends, they followed a long straight section and could see lights coming towards them and thought, 'these lights are on the wrong side of the road!'

Then realised it was him driving on the right instead of the left! He quickly pulled over to the correct side of the road just as a large Juggernaut went flying past and he thought. 'Goodness me! How long had he been driving on the wrong side of the road?' he then realise it was after getting petrol and leaving the garage around four or five miles back and before going around those bends.

He felt so bad he had to stop, and was violently sick at the thought of what could have happened, had he met the truck on the bends. It would have gone right over them and kept going! God must certainly have been watching over them that night as Gerald's wife, baby son Graham and himself would have been no more, and our their lovely Grandchildren, Larrisa and Brandon, would never have been born. It really doesn't bear thinking about, and of course, he would not be writing this book for me today. Graham is now 43 and sadly the Morris Mini has gone to that Great scrapyard in the sky.

This picture was taken when they came home from Germany to show Graham off to their Family, in Slimbridge at that time.

This is Gerald and june's son Graham, left picture Graham around five or six months old and there first new car and Graham actually learned to drive in it when he was old enough, around nineteen, see right picture.

Mini Revival

A man who bought a Mini car 18 years ago in West Germany, but sold it soon after has bought it again ----- after spotting it in Tesco's car Park in Quedgeley! Gerald Griffiths bought the car for £414 in 1967 from the manufacture's factory in Cologne, West Germany, when he was stationed there in the Grenadier Guards. Gerald of the Rea Bridge House, Elmore Lane Quedgeley, sold it two years later to a couple in Stroud after bringing it over from West Germany, Gerald, the Bridge keeper thought that was the last he would see of the first car he had ever bought.

But to his amazement he spotted 20 years later in Tesco's car park in Quedgeley--- and later bought it from Mrs Pauline Lambert of Berkeley Close, Cashes Green, Stroud, for £175. Gerald plans to use it to teach his son Graham (19) to drive. The car is still in good working order and Gerald plans to work on it to keep it in tip top condition. Gerald said it was the first brand new car that I ever bought. When I saw it again in the car park at Quedgeley I recognised it immediately'"

CHAPTER TWELVE

Well as you can see from this draft from an Australian news paper, Gerald and June are going to move to Australia, as and when they get permission to go. So it looks like that I hope to be going with them, I am sure Gerald would not have gone to all the trouble of getting me Resurrected (Restored). So see you down under, in OZ.

Hi Gerald, I hope all is well. I thought I'd send you a rough draft of your story for Emigrate to Australia, so you can check the information is correct. Feel free to let me know if there is anything you're not happy about. Also, will you be able to send me a picture for use alongside the article? Regards, David

It may have taken him a little longer than the rest of his family to decide that Australia is where his future lay, but 68-year-old Gerald Griffiths is determined to prove that when it comes to immigrating to Australia, age is no barrier.

"I already have one brother and two sisters out in Australia at the moment, while my son and grandchildren also live out there," says Gerald. "I did have two brothers out there at one point, but one has sadly passed away."

Having relatives living in different parts of Australia—his brother and one of his sisters live in Sydney, the other sister resides in Adelaide while his son is in Brisbane—means that Gerald, who has visited the country on five previous occasions, has seen various parts of Oz over the years, but it is Brisbane where he is intending to settle, close to his son and grandchildren.

So what has suddenly prompted him to make the move Down Under? "My wife, June, and I have now retired from our day jobs, and it just feels like the right thing for us to do," he answers.

While emigrating will mean the Griffiths' will have to sell their treasured house beside the Rea Bridge in Gloucester—a gift from the Waterways for whom Gerald worked as a Bridge man for 23 years up until the age of 50—the couple are really excited about starting the next chapter of their life. "We are getting on in years, but we're not too old to make this great decision," he says.

The couple are currently going through the process of obtaining a Parent visa, with their son, obviously, as the sponsor, and a nephew—one of Gerald's sister's sons—acting as the assuror of support.

"We considered going through the process alone as it should be quite straightforward," explains Gerald. "But in the end we decided to use a migration agent as it would be a lot easier and take the pressure off us.

"Our agent came recommended by a director of GR Lanes Health Products, a company I used to work for, who emigrated a couple of years ago. I figured that he was a businessman who knew what he was talking about so this would be a good enough recommendation."

So, has he been happy with the level of support he has received to date?

"I've found the agents very helpful," Gerald responds. "To be honest I haven't really had to do anything. It's just been a case of sign here, sign there and let them get on with it. We've even been provided with a list of recommendations by the agency for other companies we could consider using for other stages of the process, such as removals.

"The only frustrating thing about the whole process really is the waiting".

Gerald and June hope to be out in Australia by the end of next summer, and are counting down the days. However, while at 68 years of age you could forgive Gerald for simply wanting to put his feet up and enjoy his retirement amid his new, warmer surroundings, nothing could be further from the truth.

"I'm planning to open up my own martial arts dojo out there," explains Gerald, who has been practising martial arts, mostly karate and tai chi along with various weapon-based disciplines, for over 40 years. He is currently the chief instructor for Shotos Traditional Karate Kai—practising Shoto-Kai and Shoto-Kai forms of karate—in Gloucester.

"I've been interested in martial arts ever since my days in the Grenadier Guards many years ago," he tells me. "I was in the armed forces for nine years and three years on reserves during which time I became very keen on unarmed combat, learning how to disarm people carrying knives and so on."

It's even possible that Gerald's interest in martial arts during his time in the forces rubbed off on a future monarch. "In 1962 the late King Hussein of Jordan and I were on manoeuvres together," recalls Gerald. "He was impressed with some of my knife throwing and how I could make them stick in trees from distances and asked me how I did it.

"A few years later I saw in one of the combat magazines I buy that he had achieved a black belt in karate. I like to think I contributed to this in some way," he adds with a laugh.

As yet Gerald admits that he hasn't really looked into possible locations for his based dojo, and that he is waiting until they arrive in Australia before he starts to look. He has, however, been thinking about what it will look like.

"There's a gym under JJB Sports in Gloucester that's very impressive," he says. "I've taken a few photos of it to give me some ideas."

Not that Gerald is planning on making a living from the dojo. "It'll be used for a hobby rather than a business," he explains. "I'm probably a bit too old to be getting involved in all the bits and pieces you need to operate a business, so it's just something for me, and a few friends to use.

"Of course, if it starts to take off I'll consider starting it as a business, but . . . well, we'll see." For now, though, Gerald and June only have their sights on getting the visas that will enable them to join the various other members of their family in Oz.

"Our life will be just starting," states Gerald. "We are just so excited about it.

Gerald's Emigration plans to Australia are completed and all Visas are signed and sealed and Gerald plans to move to South Australia, to be closer to wonderful family members there, a Nephew and his wife, and there family, also a Niece and her husband and family. Which is in south Australia near Adelaide

On arriving in Oz, Gerald and June was made very welcome and stayed in Seaford for a few weeks, eventually moving to Aldinga Beach. Gerald and June started to settle down while waiting for all their belongings and of course me.

Well I first arrived in Port Adelaide South Australia on or around the 19th of July 2010 with Wridgways a Worldwide Mover, my trip was as far as I know uneventful, a bit rough some of the way, 'but well cars don't get sea-sick', so I was OK, I was at sea around two and a half months locked in a Container with the whole of Gerald's belongings which was 188 packages, plus me.

They delivered the ship's Container off to Gerald and June's after some time after I arrived, as all the consignment had to be inspected for any pests or diseases which could pose a threat to Australia.

what with Quarantine and so much paperwork that had to be done regarding me, Gerald had to come and collect me himself, and all the Paper work and forms had to be correct what with the Registration and Tax's ECT; So Gerald was not able to collect me until 19th October 2010, which was nearly three months after I arrived, I was kept in the Customs Hall at Port Adelaide all that time.

CHAPTER THIRTEEN

Before I arrived Gerald took charge of his Brother's Car that he had bought off his Brothers estate when his brother Andrew Bryant Griffiths had died in 2007 of Cancer, Andrew had lived in Australia for quite a number of years, Gerald bought it as he wanted to keep it in the family, as this car was a Classic just like me, and Andrew called it Rupert as in 'Rupert the Rover', for Rupert was a 1974 Rover 2000 and had been restored with dedication and love by Andrew.

Andrew Bryant Griffiths 1947-2007.   Andrew had Rupert this Classic Car for some time.

As you can see Rupert is in immaculate condition and Andrew took great pride in looking after it, just like Gerald is now looking after me . . .

Rupert the Rover 2012. At Aldinga Beach, and still looking like new.

These photos were taken before I arrived in Australia as Gerald was using Rupert as his everyday car. The photos were taken at Aldinga Beach Esplanade, Eastside, towards Silver sands and sellicks Beach, which you can see in the distant.

Silver Sands Beach, Eastside of Aldinga.

This Beach is over looking Maslin Beach Westside of Aldinga.

CHAPTER FOURTEEN

VEHICLE IMPORT APPROVAL

Regional Development and Local Government

MOTOR VEHICLE STANDARDS ACT 1989

Mr Gerald Glyn Griffiths
The Rea Bridge House
Elmore Lane West
Quedgeley Gloucester GL2 3NW
UNITED KINGDOM

Approval: 107274/1

IMPORT APPROVAL ISSUED UNDER REGULATION 17 - MOTOR VEHICLE BUILT BEFORE 1 JANUARY 1989

I approve the importation of the vehicle(s) described in the Schedule below under regulation 17 of the Motor Vehicle Standards Regulations and section 20(1)(b) of the *Motor Vehicle Standards Act 1989* (the Act) on the basis that the vehicle(s) was manufactured before 1 January 1989.

Approval is given, under section 17A of the Act, for you to take delivery of the vehicle.

Please note the vehicle is not exempt from State or Territory registration requirements. You should determine such requirements from the motor vehicle registration authority in the State or Territory where you intend to register the vehicle.

An application may be made to the Administrative Appeals Tribunal for a review of this decision or you may request, under section 28 of the *Administrative Appeals Tribunal Act 1975*, reasons for my decision. Any applications or requests should be made within 28 days of receipt of this notice.

I am the person authorised under section 23 of the Act to make these approvals in relation to section 17A and regulation 17.

Administrator of Vehicle Standards
18 September 2009

SCHEDULE

No.	Year	Make	Model	VIN/Chassis No.
1	1964	Morris	Minor	MAS1D1064685

Page 1 of 1

Department of Infrastructure, Transport, Regional Development and Local Government GPO Box 594 Canberra ACT 2601 Telephone: 1800 815 272 Facsimile: (02) 6274 601

Import approval document for Moggy.

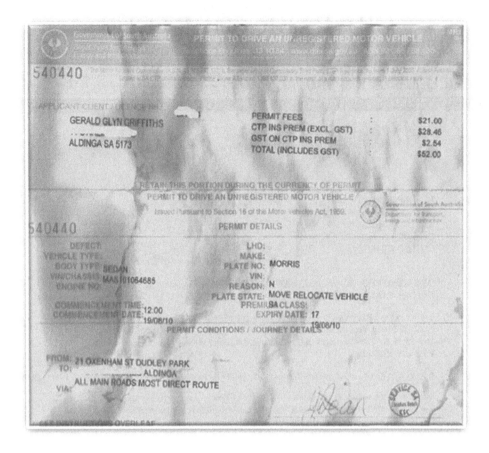

Today is the 19th August 2010 above is the permit for Gerald to be able to drive me; a Unregistered Motor Vehicle on the road, and I am now waiting at 21 Oxen ham St Dudley Park at the Customs in Port Adelaide in South Australia for Gerald to pick me up to take me home to his house in a place called Aldinga Beach.

Gerald arrived later that day, a close friend was able to drive him here, 'I was very thrilled to see him'. When he started me up I almost started straight away, as the Customs know he was coming and put my battery on charge. Gerald was talking to the custom's men, and they said they loved seeing a great car like a Morris Minor, in so good condition, they said it made there day.

After Gerald got me home, I still could not be driven anywhere, as I had to be registered, and to do this I had to be put over a pit to show I was road worthy and be checked that the paperwork corresponded with my body and Heart (*Engine*) numbers. So Gerald had to apply again for a temporary permit to take me there at a later date.

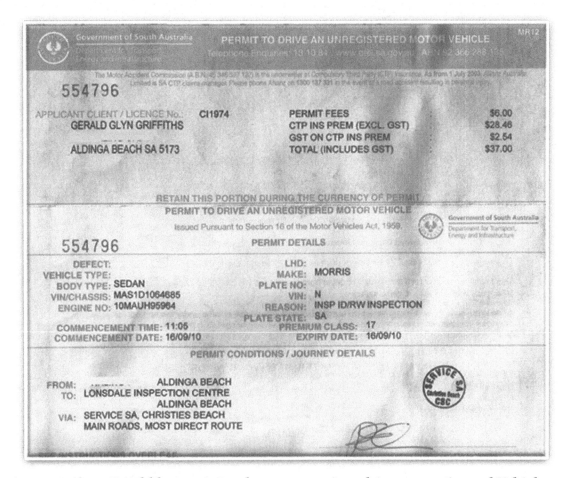

As you can see Gerald has now got the new permit to drive a unregistered Vehicle to take me to the Lonsdale inspection Centre in Lonsdale about thirty miles away. This picture is my first home in OZ, and I was garaged.

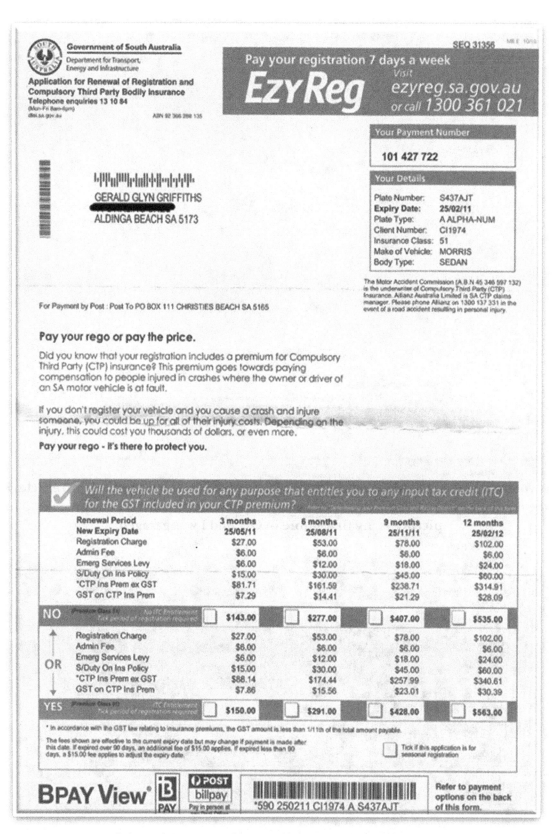

I am now taxed, 'Rego', as Australians call it, my new number plate is: S437-AJT

Date Printed: 4 March 2011
Client/Licence Number: **CI1974**
Payment Number: 101427722

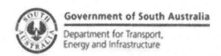
Government of South Australia
Department for Transport,
Energy and Infrastructure

GERALD GLYN GRIFFITHS
44 STIRLING CRES
ALDINGA BEACH SA 5173

**SAFETY AND REGULATION
DIVISION**
ABN 92 366 288 135

GPO Box 1533
Adelaide SA 5001
Telephone: 13 10 84

REMINDER NOTICE
VEHICLE REGISTRATION HAS EXPIRED

When this letter was prepared the MORRIS SEDAN with registration **S437AJT** expired on 25/02/11.

Immediate payment of your registration is required if you wish to use the above vehicle. It is an offence to drive an unregistered vehicle and penalties apply.

If you have since paid and renewed the registration, please disregard this notice.

You can quickly and easily renew your registration using one of the following convenient payment options:

- By visiting www.ezyreg.sa.gov.au, clicking on "renew your registration now" and paying using your credit card
- by phoning 1300 361 021 and following the prompts
- Over the counter at any Registration & Licencing or Service SA Centre
- By sending a cheque or money order payment via mail to: "Registration Renewal" PO BOX 111 CHRISTIES BEACH SA 5165

Note: You must not drive the vehicle until payment of the registration renewal has been received and processed.

Payment made up to 90 days after the expiry date will not have the expiry date adjusted unless a higher administration fee is paid and it is requested by you. Payments made 90 or more days after the expiry date will automatically be charged a higher administration fee* and the expiry date will be adjusted.

If you are unsure of the fees payable to renew your registration please visit www.ezyreg.sa.gov.au or phone 13 10 84 and speak with one of our friendly customer service operators during the hours of 8am to 6pm Monday to Friday.

If you no longer require registration of this vehicle or if the vehicle has been sold, wrecked, written off or defected, please phone 13 10 84.

Yours Sincerely,

Martin Small

REGISTRAR OF MOTOR VEHICLES

Sequence No: 6921

*Seasonal registrations are excluded. A vehicle may be registered as "Seasonal" if vehicle use is only for part of the year. For more information regarding Seasonal registration, please contact the Customer Service Centre on 13 10 84.

You get these notice reminders when the tax gets to run out.

CHAPTER FIFTEEN

On arriving in Australia this was my first home, which is in Aldinga Beach, South Australia Gerald and June loved it here in this home and they lived there for about a year and half, during this time I went out on regular trips to the Beach and to the next town called, Seaford,

This is my second home, still in Aldinga but only ten houses away from the beach.

This is me at the top of our road on the Esplanade, in Aldinga. Well I am back from the inspection Centre and passed with flying colours, they were very impressed of how good the condition of how I looked. Gerald is really pleased and has taken me for a nice long drive along the Sea front at Aldinga where we live; the scenery is beautiful, as we cruised along the esplanade, going through Aldinga beach and into Sellicks beach a few miles away. Gerald and June loved going up along this esplanade as the view's are fantastic and they go walking along the beach, Gerald would go running along the beach for his fitness as he is a Martial arts instructor and likes to keep up his fitness and stamina.

This is part of the beach Gerald go's running, and in the top picture, he runs along the top of the esplanade to the left of the picture and runs down some ninety steps, comes back along the beach from the left of the picture, then back up the steps you see in this picture and there are well over seventy steps of which he do's not stop till he gets to the top.

These are the steps he runs down, along the beach to the other steps that we seen on the last page.

A beautiful Sunset from the top of the steps

These Photos has been taken at the Maslin Beach lookout, overlooking the first official nudist beach in Australia.

In these Photos Gerald and June are at the beach in a place called Moana, this beach is a favourite for Surfers, and is usually packed. In this area is a surf and life saving club, a Pub and a fitness centre? I love these little trips with June and Gerald, and I get to see the beaches and the countryside.

The last three photos are Moana Beach, and Moana is just along the Esplanade from Seaford.

The picture below is Gerald out on a leisure drive with Rupert at Silver Sands, he had just taken me for a drive to keep me ticking over and was now doing the same for Rupert the Rover, it's really good because we are never taken for very, very long drive's, which would wear us out, they are more leisurely so we are never hammered or driven into the ground, so we are well looked after, cleaned and polished every few weeks, so we are gleaming all the time, and showed off at Motor shows ECT. Gerald is so proud of us.

This is me on the Beach you have just seen Rupert the Rover in the last picture, called, 'Silver Sands'. I am actually on the beach, and the picture below I am overlooking the beach with June, Gerald's wife sitting in my passenger seat while he takes my picture.

These Photos, I am at Christy's Beach in the background where the cliffs are there is an R.S.L. club which would be the same as the British Legion in Britain. Gerald use to do a Disco and cabaret at this Club, he enjoys this as he is quite a good singer. This is the Memorial Garden and a photo of a war time cannon, outside the R.S.L. club.

CHAPTER SIXTEEN

In a lot of places in Australia, you will see these signs along the roads, Gerald loves these, we were going along when he starts laughing and were pointing them out to June, hahaha, and the first one, don't drive like a Knob, and don't drive like a wanker, and a cock. There are lots of speeding signs as well, where there is a large picture of a Policeman's head with him wearing dark glasses, as all Cop's wear them, he is pointing at you, and the word on the board says, 'we are watching you'. So don't speed in Oz. There are also signs saying, 'Don't Creep'.

The roads in Australia can be as straight as straight, to the horizon; these two pictures would be about five or six miles away and as flat and as straight as far as the eye can see. You could be driving on these for hours and hours and not see anything, not even another car.

So you wonder why people speed, thank God Gerald has an everyday car, so I don't have to be driven on these long, long journeys, being a Classic car of over forty eight years old, My Forty Ninth Birthday will be in the year 2014, I am really too old and wouldn't want these long drive's. Since being in Australia, Gerald has been on about six of these long drives, nearly every time he went on them, he was done for speeding.

He has driven from South Australia, right up to Queensland on two occasions and up to New-South-Wales four times', Queensland and back would be around five thousand miles. He has a three and a half litre Mitribushi Magna which is a very fast car, this picture is Gerald's Magna,

The Police cars are very sophisticated with very high-tech equipment on board, Police car could be coming towards you, five or six miles away, and if you are speeding, they would have recorded you before you could even see them in the distant. So as a nice little Classic car my advice to you is do not speed however strait the roads are, if you speed you will be caught.

This is Gerald and June on a trip to Victor harbour, which is a beautiful seaside town, with a beautiful island called Granite Island, where you can go on trips to by a horse drawn carriage on a railway line.

CHAPTER SEVENTEEN

One of the most amazing things that happened to Gerald was, he was giving me a wash and polish in his back garden, when all these wild Rainbow Lorikeet's flew into the tree's around are house and the neighbour's house next door, there must have been about fifty of them, 'quite noisy'. Then we heard are neighbour calling, 'Gerald, Gerald', come and see this, when Gerald went around to the fence, his neighbour, Roger had a Rainbow Lorikeet on his shoulder, he said it had flown down out of the tree's on to his shoulder and was chatting and kissing him, He said wow, 'that's brill', He went nearer the fence and Roger said, call him Gerald, he did and it flew on to the fence and then on to his shoulder, then it was chatting away to him. It was 'fantastic and amazing' Here is the proof to prove it, from photos from his video camera. 'Amazing'. The first picture is Roger in his garden after he called him, the trees behind him and in Gerald's garden was covered with them.

Here he is coming over the fence towards Gerald, look at the beautiful colours, know wonder they call them Rainbow Lorikeet's. For they do look just like the colours of the Rainbow.

He is just about land on Gerald's shoulder, Gerald was so lucky to have had his camera with him, he was going to take a picture of me after he cleaned me, and having this happen, had made his day

On my little car trips out with Gerald and June, we have seen so many beautiful Bird's, the parrot's are so much in abundance in Australia, we were down in Port'Norlunga near Aldinga, where we live and in the trees by the Sports ground without exaggeration there were about a thousand White Cockatoo's in the tree's, it was amazing and so colourful.

In the tree's it looked like white Blossoms covering the whole of the trees, and all over the ground, they were everywhere. On the mainland of Australia, Galahs are found in all of the states, from the North to the South, but not so many in the far north and the Driest areas, but there is still very much an endemic of them.

There are many verities of Galahs, from Rose-breasted Cockatoo's, *(Eolophus roseicapilla)*, Roseate Cockatoo's, Galahs Cockatoo's, the most common being the Pink and gray. They can be found in rural townships and are abundant in the open countryside's. One of the most colourful parrots is the Rainbow Parakeets and Lorikeets, one of them is smaller than the other, and I think the Parakeets are much smaller, more like a Budge.

This picture was taken just at the top of our road in Aldinga, only a few houses from Gerald's Mate Simon Cunningham, a guy who Emigrated from Ireland a few years ago, he worked away a lot and Gerald helped him out by his Garden up together while he is away

CHAPTER EIGHTEEN

For a while now we have been excited waiting for Geralds best friend, Tony and his future Wife, 'Kate', to come out to Ausralia, for a visit. This is a lovely Picture Kate took of Tony, Gerald and June, when Gerald and June picked them up from the Airport in Adelaide.

The next picture is of Gerald's best friend Tony and his Girlfriend Kate enjoying their holiday, Tony has had a drive in both of us Car's that's Rupert and myself, and he loved us, but Gerald has used his Mitsubishi Magna to drive them around, he took them to the lookout, over-looking Maslin Beach, and a few other places in and around Aldinga and the sea front by are home.

Gerald also took them to Victor Harbour, which is about thirty miles from Aldinga, a favourite place Gerald and June likes to go, in the picture behind them is a horse drawn railway carriage.

The horse pulls it along a railway line along a woodened jetty, bridge over to an Island called Granite Island, on this Island you can see the Seals and Penguins swimming around the Island, there is also a Restaurant overlooking the Island, with rocks, and beautiful beach views that you can see that are along the mainland.

The next picture is June; Gerald's wife on Granite Island and the Horse-drawn carriage making its way off the Island towards the mainland. Gerald was saying that it is quite sad really, as these horses are on a alternating change around, and are working nearly all day, in sweltering heat of 42 degree.

CHAPTER NINETEEN

This picture is the jetty railway line and Granite Island.

There were many other places; we went to, like Glenelg, which is a beautiful seaside town, where there are a lot of tourist. We also went to Adelaide, and also on a Dolphins cruise at Port Adelaide. On the cruise which last about two to three hours, and a beautiful lunch on board in the restaurant, while looking out the windows for the Dolphins.

'Right', 'Well', Gerald has put Kate and Tony in my book because; After they came down here in OZ, Tony asked Gerald to be his Best man at his wedding; of course Gerald agreed and was very proud to have been asked, so 10th April of this year of 2012, Gerald and June flew to England to be his Best man, at his wedding, Gerald found it very emotional with all his friends at home and with his relatives' all wanting him to stay, and in this next picture is Gerald with Tony in England Gerald as Best Man, he was very proud to have been, Gerald said it was such an honour.

Part of the Best-Man's duty, was to deliver a speech for the Groom and to toast the Bride and Groom, in doing so to wish them a fabulous life together, ECT; Gerald found this very hard to do as he was overcome by the lovely gift Tony and Kate presented to him, Tony and Kate presented Gerald with a lovely original picture of the Battle Honours of The Grenadier Guards that they bought at a Grenadier Guards function the year before, which was Auction on the evening and. Gerald is holding it in the picture above, this made him very emotional and humbled, and this was just before his speech, because of this Gerald found this very hard, which actually made his speech that much more endearing. 'This is Gerald's speech'.

Bride & Groom Tony & Kate Lady's & Gentleman, My name is Gerald Griffiths.

I have had a very privileged life so far, as I had served in the armed forces for twelve years as an honored member of the Queens personal Guards, (The Grenadier Guards) A regiment of great epic proportions of outstanding privileges and esteem to HER MAJASTY THE QUEEN. I have had some very privileged proud moments of being part of some very important ceremonies, which I was so honored to be present at, on so many numerous occasions.

But today is one of my most proud moments and honored to be asked by Tony to be his best man today.

I remember the very first time I met Tony, it was at a place where I worked, he had started work there the same time, which is so funny as Tony now only lives just around the corner of the factory where we worked, which is G. R. Lanes at the back of his house, I warmed to Tony as soon as we met, he is such a likeable man. We were talking about my Martial Arts and where I instructed, he showed much interest to what I had to say, to cut a long story short, he became one of our club members and over a few short years with dedication, his martial arts became outstanding and he achieved and was awarded his first Dan Black Belt on the 15th of November 2009.

As we all know when we are young sometimes we do daft and foolish things, and I remember when a delegation of Martial art instructors which included myself and club members which included Tony, Tony was a lot younger then. We were all invited to go to America to tour and teach in Pennsylvania. After one of our teaching training sessions at the end of the day, we were all in the Gym (DOJO) having food and drink (plenty of SPIRITS); Then we all went from there to the Pub, and I must say I was quite pissed. 'Not sure if I should have said that'; I mean I was Drunk.

Gerald Griffiths

But Tony was as pissed as the PREVERBEUL NEWT. It was so funny as at the pub and him being so drunk, he actually asked one of the top American Martial arts Instructors outside for a punch-up. I was asked to have a word with Tony and after things calmed down we all had a good laugh about it and Tony was so embarrassed.

JUST AMAGIN ASKING OUT A TOP INSTRUCTOR FOR A PUNCH-UP.

I was so pleased when Tony met Kate and I could see the Love and affection that they had for each other. Today I am so happy for them. I can see the same affections and love that my wife JUNE and I have for each other. June and I have been Married for over forty six years, I feel that Kate and Tony will go forwards to experience these same wonderful qualities we have. As I know that you all know of Kate's talent of her acting dramatics and singing abilities, and I am sure that they will have a wonderful exciting life together. I would do anything for Tony and Kate, even go right around the World for them.

'OH YES I JUST DID THAT'.

From the bottom of the World in OZ seeing these two very wonderful close friends in my life, Tony and Kate and getting to see them getting married.

118

CHAPTER TWENTY

When Gerald and June came back home to Australia from Tony and Kate's wedding, on the 2nd May, they had lots of different emotions, and factors, building up within them, they talked it over and decided to go back home to live in their lovely bungalow in England, which they could not sale because of the recession and with the exchange rate being so bad and paying rent in Australia, they decided they would be financially so much better off in England. It was very heart rendering for them as their Son and Grandchildren were still in Australia, and of course Gerald's Sister, Sheila and Brother Peter and their families, it would mean not being able to see them as often. All though Peter and Sheila lived a very long way from where Gerald and June lived Aldinga Beach South Australia.

On the upside of everything they had a lot more relatives in England and would be living very much nearer to every one of them, but even then, it is very hard when you are torn between family members. There was always a chance that their Son, Graham would return to England sometime in the future, which helped them towards some of their decisions.

These lovely photo's of, Graham, with Larrisa and Brandon, Larrisa is very beautiful as you see here and so successful in all she has done, she is a very high ranking manager at MacDonald's in Brisbane, Brandon is a very accomplished horse rider and has an apprenticeship as a Racing jockey with a very high ranking racing farm, in Nairne near Mt'Barker in the Adelaide Hill's. Just before they returned to England, Gerald and June was able to see Brandon training and going on his first full Gallop, Gerald and June are so proud of their Son and Grandchildren, and Gerald and June will find it hard going back to England, and will miss them dreadfully.

Brandon on his first training gallop.

Larrisa at twenty years old.   Brandon on his fifteenth birthday.

From this Book about my life as Moggy the Morris Minor, Gerald and June want larrisa and Brandon to know they Love them very much, and are sorry they are going back to England, and want them to know, they will never forget them, and will try and see them soon. XXX

CHAPTER TWENTY ONE

Getting ready to go Home to England

This is me, 'Moggy and Rupert', whom I have now become close friends and hope to be for the rest of our days. We all ready to go home and I am as excited as the recovery truck has just turned up and will be loading myself and Rupert in a moment, and will go to Port-Adelaide the Wridgways depot. All of Gerald and June's belongings has already gone ahead to the depot, and they almost have to camp out in their own home, till they fly out themselves. I am not looking forward though to being concealed in a container for six weeks; at least I will have Rupert as company.

We are now loaded and setting off

Nearly there.

We have arrived at the Wridgways Removalists container Warehouse. Gerald and June's Container is here waiting with all their belongings already packed, and waiting for me and Rupert, I am so disappointed as there is no room for Rupert in the same container as me, he will have to be going in a separate container, aaaawwww, so this long journey will be soooo, lonely for both of us.

They put me in my container with all Gerald and June's belonging's at least I can keep an eye on everything for them, I have been strapped down, so I will not be able to move which I know it is for my own safety, so I will not be thrown around at sea, I am not looking forwards to that, all that movement making me sea sick.

You can see that I am well tied down and wooden wedges to keep my wheels from moving.

Also you can see the size of the 40ft container, Gerald's belonging's is half to three quarters of it and I am in the other.

This is Rupert's container, which is a 22ft container, as you see Rupert has been put in and about to be roped down so he can't move for his own safety.

This was one of the Forman who were seeing to our security and putting us in the containers, he was saying his good-by's, so we say farewell to the Removers of WridgWays, and will be looking forward to seeing the guy, s at John Mason's in Great-Britain when we get there, in Croydon

CHAPTER TWENTY TWO

Trip to Peter and Shirley's

Hi'ya this is Gerald telling the story at the moment, as Moggy and Rupert has gone to England. We will not be able to follow them as yet, we would not have anywhere to go, and the bungalow in Britain is at the moment rented, so we cannot move in yet. We will be following in a month's time; it will take Moggy and Rupert six weeks to get there, so we will be there when they arrive. June and I are going to drive down to see my brother in New South Wale's a place called Goulburn, as are house is now empty, it is a round trip of three thousand miles, and we are going for five maybe six days. I have done this trip five or six times before, since being in Australia, so should be use to it by now.

I am telling you about this trip as there was some very interesting things regarding old transport, I found this very interesting because of my interest in Classical Car's, also my Brother, Graham Senior was very interested with this subject as well. We passed through a small town near Melbourne and we came across a Cafe and it was called Cobb's Cafe, now going back into the history of Cobb's and Co, you will find it goes right back to the days of the Stage couches of the Wild-West, and also when they first came to Australia all those years ago.

This is my Mitsubishi Magna actually outside the Cobb's Cafe;

The Town is called Murryville in Victoria, 19 Mckenzie Street, and is own by a nice young couple Rebecca Noble, and David Quinn. 'The way to go is Cobb & Co'. The Cafe had old Pictures of yesteryear on the walls which was quite historic and very interesting. Around the 19th Century a small group of immigrants from America, a Mister Freeman Cobb, John Murray Peck, John B Lamber and a James Swanton, set up Cobb's Company in Melbourne, Victoria 1853.

The Cobb's Company became very successful, originally the Company was called, The American Telegraph Line of Coaches. The success of the Company was mostly due to the fact that the expansion of settlers and pastoral settlements right across Australia, and the Country's growth of mining of various minerals and Gold, ECT;

The company supplied pioneering transport of routes and trails around vast areas of Australia, delivering Mail and Gold. The first passenger coach who set off from Melbourne on 30th January 1854, to a place called Forest Creek which is now called (Castlemaine) and Bendigo. The routes and links to goldfields and settlements, from this Cobb's company was awarded increasing mail contracts and were able to operate gold escorts, passengers and mail services throughout Australia.

So goodbye to Cobb's Cafe; Now on to another town on route, there was a lovely Bridgeman's cottage, and I thought of our home we had in England at the, 'Rea Bridge House', and being an ex Bridgeman myself it was so nice to see, we had a nice walk around the village, it was so nice, we decided to stay overnight, of course on these long journeys you need to stop and rest at least every two hours anyway.

This was all on the way to Goulburn, a beautiful Bridgeman's Cottage, there is June standing under the sign that say's, 'The Bridgeman Cottage'. We stayed at a Motel here, which was very comfortable, and such a lovely village to walk around.

There was lovely cottage's and fields and a beautiful Shire-Horse, probably like the horse's Cobb's Company would have used, pulling there Stage-couches years ago. This photo is June looking at him in his field, with a small poney.

Just driving to Peter and Shirley's home, on stretches of our trip, the sunsets were amazing,

When you arrive in Goulburn, you will see this huge ram, which is in fact a Wool Shop. Which is a huge landmark, and very popular with the tourists, it has about three floors, and has a restaurant and wool shop with lots of memorabilia. Lots of wool rug's and carpet's and Sheepskin rug's ECT;

This is the first place, where you can see my Brothers home, it is a beautiful place high up on this hill, on the horizon, and in the centre there are three clumps of tree that is his place.

In the top two Pic's June and Shirley, then Peter and myself, then this picture is; left to right, Peter's son, Jesse, Gerald, June, and Peter's daughter Amy and Peter.

This is a beautiful sunset at Peter and Shirley's, and my Car in the forground.

Goodbye to Australia see you again soon.

Like they say, A Boomerang always comes back, and I have one with me,
so see you again soon.

We are now going back home, I am going to hand you back to Moggy.

CHAPTER TWENTY THREE

Moggy here; Arriving at John Mason's in Croydon, England and Gerald's home.

Well Rupert and I have arrived in Great-Britain, at John Mason's in Croydon and were there at the depot a week before Gerald was able to come and pick us up. He is here and is driving this recovery truck, we have been loaded and will be on our way, but first this young man in the picture I befriended, wanted to have his picture taken with me.

I have been taken to Gerald and June's House, and parked in his drive, the next day Gerald drove back to Croydon to fetch Rupert, I bet he must be knackered with all this driving as it is about two hundred miles round trip, any way I can hear them arrive and Gerald is just going to unload Rupert and take the truck back to the people he hired it from.

Well this is Gerald's home and it is a lovely Bungalow, and as you can see, we have a two space parking area, and will be covered with our covers. I cannot wait to have a look around and maybe go and see Teresa, Ellen and Leanne, maybe surprised them.

That could be my next sequel, bye for now, keep an eye out for me on the road.

Lots of Love to
Everyone
from
MOGGY

John & Teresa Griffiths a ring pulls stringing record attempt for National kidney

Research, a news paper cutting of John with only 19 miles to go.

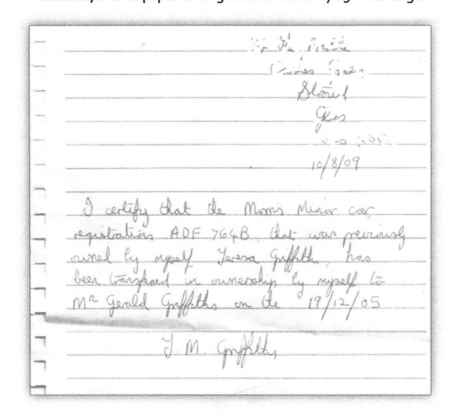

Gerald and June in their Beach buggy.

This is a photo of Gerald with his good Lady, June.

The book of Moggy will be a lovely keepsake for their Grandchildren. But Gerald has just importantly has Written his Autobiography of his life, so his Grandchildren will have and be able to know of the wonderful qualities of his Mother and Father, brothers and sisters, and the love he has for them, plus those no longer with us, he miss'ies them dreadfully. he wanted to be able to give his own Son and Grandchildren a keepsake they would be able to cherish for years to come come, and hopefully show their children, and their childrens, children, the life of their Great Great Grandparents. Please look out for this book as it is a lovely read of a wonderful family.

Also Gerald has published a Book on his Martial Arts. See front covers of both books.

Book on the left,
The Auto Biography of an
Ex Grenadier Guardsmen.
On the right
Shoto's Traditional Karate Kai.